Franciscan

Notes

◆

ALAN WILLIAMSON

FRANCISCAN

NOTES

TUPELO PRESS
North Adams, Massachusetts

Franciscan Notes.
Copyright © 2019 Alan Williamson.
All rights reserved.

First edition: October 2019.

Library of Congress Cataloging-in-Publication Data available upon request.

ISBN: 978-1-946482-25-9

COVER ART:
Cimabue, "Black Crucifixion", circa 1277-80, fresco.
Upper Church, San Francesco, Assisi.

*Cover and text designed and composed
in Adobe Minion by Dede Cummings.*

Other than brief excerpts for reviews and commentaries, no part of this book
may be reproduced by any means without permission of the publisher. Please
address requests for reprint permission or for course-adoption discounts to:

TUPELO PRESS
P.O. BOX 1767, NORTH ADAMS, MASSACHUSETTS 01247
(413) 664–9611 / editor@tupelopress.org / www.tupelopress.org

Tupelo Press is an award-winning independent literary press that publishes
fine fiction, nonfiction, and poetry in books that are a joy to hold as well as
read. Tupelo Press is a registered 501(c)(3) nonprofit organization, and we rely
on public support to carry out our mission of publishing extraordinary work
that may be outside the realm of the large commercial publishers. Financial
donations are welcome and are tax deductible.

Produced with support from the National Endowment for the Arts

ART WORKS.
arts.gov

Once again, for Jeanne and for Elizabeth.

◆

CONTENTS

♦ *I* ♦

A Sick Child   3

For My Mother   4

After Oral Surgery   6

The Death of Picasso   7

The Psychopomps   9

Summer Afternoon in the South   10

New Orleans Poem   11

San Francisco Grand Ball: Airport Marriott   13

Jojo Listens to Gotterdammerung   16

The Ring   17

Poems of Summer   20

After Caravaggio   22

Toward Retirement   24

Event Horizon   27

Bebert   30

Bamian: A Photograph from Tricycle, 2000   31

Fantasia on a Medieval Latin Poem   32

No. 1 Piazzetta Calamandrei   35

Cathedral   36

Le Convertoie   37

Ownership   39

Oh the persimmons,   40

Sleep   41

Messengers from the Past   45

The Old Man by the Roadside   46

Leopardi: Chorus of the Dead   47

The Bharhut Gate   49

Montale at Monterosso   52

◆ *II* ◆

Franciscan Notes   55

I.

◆

A SICK CHILD

Sometimes I feel I'm a sick child forever,
too tired to carry anything through, too bed-worn
and fretful to fall asleep. The radio
helps, at certain hours. A tableau
of Chicago winter, light snow flurries, monochromes
everything outside my window. Home
from class, my father talks to me from the doorway.
He's awkward, but for once he doesn't expect of me
anything I can't do. The shadow gathers
with its particular loneliness, though elsewhere
it makes lights spark on; women put on jewels,
parties begin. But sometimes something falls
away from me in those hours: my mind grows simple,
wanting nothing, worried by nothing, imperturbable
as time. And a day will come when I'll ask my mother
for an extra meal, between lunch and supper.
She'll know I'm better then, and will supply it,
a small paté sandwich with the crusts cut off.

FOR MY MOTHER

We refused to obey the law and scatter your ashes
a full mile offshore: you had asked for the tiderocks—

chain of islets, really, off the point, where the sea explodes
most crystalline; but walkable at low water—

after a handful were buried on my father's grave.
What childhood foot-memory kept me steady, the square-

cornered box off-weighting my arms, thrown by the rocks'
tilted faces and blunt points—the hot March sun—

(But why the tiderocks? They were my place, not yours,
where our biologist friend named the new species

of nudibranch we found there, _alanii_; yet I remember you there,
sunrise-touched, uncharacteristically happy

for that summer we had to go West,
my father in the hospital; Liberty scarf round your hair—

Did you think of that, too?) The rocks' cracks and trapezoidal
jumble, revealed in the photo, a kind of grid

or graph paper to map our bent-over shapes, hair-fine—
against time, against life?—out to the far tooth

where I cast the last ashes aslant the wind, to fall
only half in water, half dusting

a nest of barnacles, to wait for the high tide . . .
Another mistake, desecration? As when I left you

the day I shouldn't, gambling the doctors were right, *no change*,
your premonition wrong . . .   The others

don't blame me, of course; and what
could it matter now, anyway?

All I can ever do for you is done.

AFTER ORAL SURGERY

Off the shadowy fake-marble corridor
of what was once "The Leamington," in downtown Oakland,
where I've left five teeth now
behind these bright doors black-stencilled
in both Chinese and English,
I think about the separability
of things from persons—
my father-in-law's black shoes
that fit my feet so neatly,
my own clothes some day a problem for survivors....

My mother's tastes that, perhaps as much as anything,
spoke for who she was, in their particulate drift
down the time-wind: the Guatemalan blankets
with two facing monkeys,
soft black on softer off-white wool, now worn
to the nub; her zircon earring,
undersea Art Deco glamour-green,
that broke, and my daughter made into a pendant...

One can understand the wish to have a bonfire
of objects as of bodies,
not go on dreaming the impossibility
of packing up my childhood room
before some vague, but very pressing, deadline....
Though, as I think in my half-somnolence,
bonfires too are gone now,
illegal, that used to gather,
at every autumn street corner, smoky leaves . . . .

THE DEATH OF PICASSO

(For Joyce Root and Guy Davenport, *in memoriam*)

The deli in Newton. Even my almost estranged
wife found something to like in me, that I went there,
building my nest on the waters, the spare half-hour
before an appointment with you; crossing a time-path,
perhaps, with your other life I couldn't know . . . .
"It's your _place_!" she exclaimed. The tables chipped formica
and tightly spaced. Often I had to share one.

And that made me a friend, one day,
or at least an acquaintance, because I brought Guy's book there,
"The Death of Picasso"—his bisexual Eden
where no shadow falls between the mind's clarity
and the body's feral suppleness—whiffs and salt-stings
of his Greek or North Sea islands,
grace-notes of "huffle" and "humpenscrump of the waves,"
and no shadow falls, too, on the sharp-focused sentences
where it becomes possible to write, one day,
"this deliciously strange feeling that time is nothing,
or is my friend rather than my enemy."

There are islands and islands. Once, in India,
I saw two beggar women stake out their places to sleep
on the stained concrete of the long platform
between railway lines. They were close enough to each other
to imply mutual protection, and far enough
to draw each her own magic circle, which the crowds
respected. Like Rousseau: the gypsy woman's
sleep as much blessed as threatened by the lion's
glassy huge eye . . . .

7

The deli *was* my place, to live without the shadow
minutes at a time. Just so
inside your voice was a space, when what you said
was so right and quiet, I didn't exactly hear it
but floated in its vibrations, under your heart . . .
Then I wanted to wear a ribbon of you and only
in the ghostly falling of hot streets, enduring
myself, I somehow could, now knowing
there was a limit I could no longer pass into non-being . . .

You gone, Guy gone . . . . Picasso's real face
in the late photo I have from Palazzo Grassi:
the tar-black eyeballs protruding from the skull
as if they saw 360 degrees, in profound suspicion
of all that might come at him, especially himself,
that minotaur—his genius perhaps
not disinhibition so much as a child's attentiveness,
the way, in *Surviving Picasso*, he makes Francoise Gilot
not stop watching the parabola of the owl stooping
on—
            whatever it is.

THE PSYCHOPOMPS

Sometimes the phone ringing just when you come in the door
is a very bad sign; a package sent back is another…

In *Boheme,* we know Mimi is gone when her music
returns in a thinner, echoless register,

but nothing breaks our featureless air at these vanishings, tricked
when our attention is turned for a wrong hour, wrong year:

Linda who won't make me feel anonymous and not-old
ever again, at some music-place on Haight or Bryant;

Joyce not to be found by two right turns at the church
in Waban, memorized in my worst year—

each bound to one body though the Buddha-pageant
of wonders rolls through us the same, as long as we're here . . .

Those we didn't say goodbye to, and can't now, demonstrating,
for once, the irremediable: in reproach or love, what matter,

they wait, and make the inconceivable "other side"
more and more surely home—

the massing of the dead at the top of the stair
in the mind that cannot accept that they are nowhere.

SUMMER AFTERNOON IN THE SOUTH

When the flash came straight down on us and cracked open
 the afternoon sleep the rain had eased me into
 untold floating minutes earlier,
 and the earth, or was it just our building, trembled;

And I thought how my mother who is dead
 taught me to count the seconds after the lightning,
 and that each one meant we were farther off, and safer,
 so hiding, from me, her own irrational fear;

And then I thought of the bark huts in the diorama
 of this place three thousand years ago; how
 the same eagle stooped and sent men running; and thought

How the immortal recombinants of fire and water
 would know no difference between then and now—
 blinking into the space where planets falter.

NEW ORLEANS POEM

(for Jeanne)

South from our winter the first sight of redbud, first dogwood
were words of an easier language; the smoky tastes were another,
gumbo file, sea-turtle; the unaccustomed courtesy

of waiters disarming an eight-year-old's
self-importance by indulging it; the Morning Call's
sugar bowls chained to the long marble bar;

the incurvings of wrought iron delighting my father so;
the austere two-toned cathedral; even the slightly
fecal street-smell found in all old cities....

City of permissions! The spring I was fourteen,
when the rain kept us in our motel room, watching the Oscars—
"Tammy" winning best song—shower-spray in the morning

gave me the hint that some Tammy might wish to twine
in the normal way around my dubious body
(so I met you, in a way, before I met you)—

It's true we owe our bodies to water, earth, air, and fire
and sky they were borrowed from; but I who stood
in this same shirt on the banks of the Ganges

watching them wedge-split the gnarled black logs for the pyres
and thought in spite of myself, *there could be worse ways to end*
(my daughter snapped my picture, as if to call me back)

stand again in this earliest moistness, following you down
the narrowing path between two bayous, spotting
the baby alligator's half-smile on a "sinker" log,

the skink's sapphire lightning, the rosebud-tipped cypress knees.

SAN FRANCISCO GRAND BALL
(AIRPORT MARRIOTT)

1.

Opposite the runways. At low tide the mudflats
stretch to a tiny trickle of reflections.
A broken chair beached halfway out, year after year.

Competitors click by. Unplanned-out time
which is also time observed by strangers.
The way your mood heaves to the height

of the glassed-in atrium, then falls
faster than you can measure or account for,
as toward some felt though unseen water-table.

You might have—no, you *did*
doze off in a place like this, after someone died,
while someone nearer used the room to phone.

2.

Sitting in this atrium is not like sitting
in the zendo. Yet, there is a weight
of Being on the potted palms, intercutting

the girders of the glass wall, that is not
the inflected weight of home, yet not
the freedom of things that grow in air. It suggests

that anyone could come from anywhere,
as the famous old poet did, after a reading,
before an early flight,

and when we recognized him, knew me only
as Jeanne's fellow dancer, not the man
who wrote that mixed review of him, long ago.

3.

Daylight severely excluded as from a bar.
Soft spotlights on the floor. Mealtimes forgotten.
Here, as Baudelaire said, the dead years do come out

on the balconies of the sky, in out-of-fashion dresses.
Their <u>own</u> fashion, anyway: flamingo-toucan,
feathers and floaters, dust-of-rhinestone spangles . . .

No music later than Sinatra. Hobbies,
as we know, like bars and churches, are alternate
worlds we create to let Time enter only

on our terms . . . though soon, to spite us all, her new
profile steps forth, chemical, stripped, imprinting
as her name in the "Dancesport" program: Hayley Toner.

4.

Your wish to set a murder mystery here—
was it a small revenge, exaggerating
the day's jealousies and overheated grudges,

Colonel Mustard with the blunt instrument in the library?
But how the uniform carpet and corridors
lent themselves to whisperings and evasions,

and how you curled up inside that, like a baby,
as if this place were a natural language for fate,
as if by locating terror here you could also

locate being at home. The planes
come in and in, with their soft settling slowing,
all night, on the facing runway.

JOJO LISTENS TO *GOTTERDAMMERUNG*

What bypassed centuries in the evolution
of human music, to make these somber ebbs and flows,
premelodic sleeps woken by flaring trumpets,
natural to you, till we wondered, *were* they nature?
You sitting still as Buddha on your chair,
ears electric-upright, who wouldn't pause
a second in your rounds for the best of Mozart....
(Loud rock sent you running for the door.)
What did you hear in them? Dear creature,
you'll take your honey-tinctured eyes, translucent
from the side, with their slight bulge, as ours aren't,
to your grave, a cat's life ahead of ours,
without telling us; or why, after nearly an hour,
you shook yourself, arced to the floor, and ambled off.

THE *RING*

The physical ordeal is part of it.
The way it trains us, night after night, to sit still
an hour longer, do with less sleep, the week
it flows beside our lives, say once a decade,
flows beside and sucks us under, even,
as if we were drawn down in Erda's dream,
where seeing what's past, and passing, and to come,
in the dark cradle of knowing
the connections, in the tangled roots of the world-ash,
is better than having to live it, step by step,
even if one's a god....

        So, cradled by
our chairs, our neighbors, the repeated sight
of the great pine-cone of the chandelier
in its earthquake netting, dimming from the top down,
the conductor's rustle-through to applause, we hear
the long-drawn E, that seems to promise building
not just a world of melodies, but the world....

So back to the god's steps. *Walkure* II,
when Wotan faces Fricka, knowing
all her real motives, but no way around her argument,
and the music catches what music, being a release,
should never catch—the shame of powerlessness,
ground down into betrayal of himself
and all he loves, until even a daughter's touch
only makes it worse....

                    Twenty-five years ago
beside my wife, but thinking of my beloved,
my life read back to me
both as Siegmund doomed and Wotan dooming,
clenched with his anger and his shame....
Shame I endured another month, before
I made my heart's wrong choice.

                        Now, I'm more likely
to see myself in Wotan as Wanderer, found on
the raggedest paths of the forest, examining
the things in himself that made it all go wrong—
not just the scheming and bad faith, but anger
that loves defiance but can't stand being defied:
Brunnhilde, Siegfried.... When he laughs
at Siegfried's ignorance of his own past,
it's the tired laugh of the old, that mocks at nothing
other than time, but has to read as mockery
to the young, who don't have anything if they don't have
the conviction that they start the world anew.
When Wotan sees his anger
again about to ruin himself and what he loves best,
it's almost in hope that he gives up the spear.

And then, as it all ebbs back
into the Rhine music, dream before the dream,
atom unsplit, gold unforged—does it teach us
that all we scheme for, shining Valhalla, will fail
because anything so perfect
must be built on a crime?
Or that love conquers all? Of course it never does,
though love's rarely been done more beautifully in its terrors
than on Brunnhilde's rock....

                    Or might the lesson
even be this: that sometimes something made
surprises us by being stronger than we are?
As an injured daughter might prove to be, or an
unrecognizing son…. We look back on ourselves
as through our own lost eye. And perhaps this rite
we've shared is, in different ways for each of us,
a kind of lost eye, as, winding to its end
on a brisk late afternoon in San Francisco,
it sends us out, our whole lives lived over,
into the blind air of every day.

POEMS OF SUMMER

Tennessee Williams's Sebastian wrote a poem each summer,
an idea that appealed to me, at fourteen.
My summers then were often the ghosts of summer,
leaving the city I loved for a fogbound coast.

It must have seemed to me, at fourteen,
a gathering of the essence, the high point of the year
I always missed, away on my fogbound coast.
So the habit, and poetry itself, became a mystery,

a distiller's essence, gathering the high point of the year
into something far more than a formula of words.
And so poetry became a mystery and a habit,
like Sebastian's way of dressing completely in white,

itself a form inexpressible in words.
I didn't see what it had to do with his being queer,
that way he had of dressing completely in white,
like an animal prepared for the sacrifice.

I didn't see what it had to do with being queer
to like opera and poetry, though my schoolmates seemed to.
Like an animal prepared for the sacrifice,
I was harried through the corridors, in those years.

Poetry, schoolmates, seemings, summer—
all gone so far away now!
Harrying him, down the alleys and the years,
the boys Sebastian had corrupted ate him alive.

All gone so far away now....
Tennessee Williams's Sebastian wrote a poem each summer,
before the boys he'd corrupted ate him alive.
My summers then were often the ghosts of summer.

AFTER CARAVAGGIO

We've talked all our lives about self-destructiveness,
how it's related to, though seeming the opposite of, the pure
quality of the alpha-male
antelope who stands in the center of the rings
of lesser males, and the females fight their way through to him.
The way, my wife said, the girl in the restaurant
kept her eyes on her boyfriend's crotch when he left the table....
Would I be thinking these things if I hadn't seen
Caravaggio's decapitated head
of Goliath, that complete gathering
of fury into every pore, as into
the bursting eyeballs—like a hanged man's erection—
the day before the mad Frenchman (why do manics
love the French Revolution?) held his Bastille Day fete?
It was in Umbria, at the bed-and-breakfast
where you'd brought your students for a ten-day workshop,
and it had gone beautifully, self-destructiveness
confined to fiction. (Is it with
or against nature that we've tried to be good men?)
But the Frenchman was the proprietor. He wanted you
to play Louis XVI. All of us a little tipsy,
as the full moon rose over his fantastical
flags and balloons; insects shrilled in the night.
A shaky ladder served for the Bastille
and the scaffold. Perched at the very summit,
your bright eyes and sharp nose underlit, crowned with darkness,
you made your grand speech in three languages.

Then the students who loved you, gentle maenads, drew
you down a step at a time. Play-falling
into their arms, miming
decapitation as hanging, with your tongue stuck out,
you seemed to recover something
of the years one could never tell what you'd do next.

TOWARD RETIREMENT

1. *The Books in My Office*

When the long year ended, and I knew I wouldn't see them
the months till fall, an almost audible sigh
passed over them, an upward riffling of their dust,
as if to say, you're free of us, or free to choose
which of us you like, to wander off in
as down a woodland path—the syllabi
and thesis chapters in the recycle bin, undetermining . . . .

Only lately they seem a waterfall
crashing down on my head, then righting itself
to crash again—the bad year this one promised
would be a good year, the project this one hinted at
never undertaken. Or the ones my eyes don't register . . . .

Who now will read *A History of Science*, its cover's
gritty-gray arcs how they saw electron orbitals
back in '43? Or crack open blue-black, twelve-inch
Rollins and Baker to *A Mirror for Magistrates*,
required reading once, when we had to learn rime royal
and Fortune's Wheel? (But *The Florida of the Inca*,
kept, once, for the old couple's sake, who gave it to me,
rides safe in the harbor of the "post-colonial.")

Oh Fortune, Fortune, how little we knew of you!

2. *Emeriti*

Why don't I visit them, even the ones I liked?
And then they're gone: the indiscreet conversation
of my first Chair's younger wife
that saved many a party—a serious Episcopalian
who systematically drank herself to death . . . .
The Irish wit with early Alzheimer's.

Is it a kind of revenge? As if to say
"I *had* to take you seriously; now I don't"
(the Catholic who inveighed against abortion,
whatever the course—a friend of Donald Davie's) . . . .
Or do I somehow blame them for all of this—
the years that keep on pushing in, like a tide,

class-lists with so many Kims, Ashleys, Briannas;
the heat; the gaseous alfalfa smell
in early June, appallingly a nostalgia
after twenty years . . . . Ah, well.
To teach at this place is life; to die in this place—
worse than life. A thought to be thrust aside.

3. *Teaching*

Easy to say, the kids weren't worth a lifework—
combing their hair in the back row, walking out
mid-class, with less than a hint of by-your-leave;
puzzled that this particular rite of passage
should stand between them and their high-paying futures . . . .
Easy, too, to praise yourself for your tenderness
toward the few in whom, year upon year,
you saw yourself, or the first beloved, rise up,
be cut down, or live one of the thousand other lives.

Shall I say, I made my time's bargain with the devil?
(while my colleague in the next room goes on insinuating
a distrust of art that won't breed little Marxists,
just more blase self-seekers . . . .)
                                        Or wrap
myself in the mystery, how any life
resolves to days, and days are always cloudy
with hazy sun of good deeds, moments focused
on one person's thought, or speech . . . . a "lifework" so forgotten

it could still be your first fall here. Look around you.
The great trees that lose their leaves, come winter,
are Valley Oaks; the others are Live Oaks.

                              And we,
who liked graduation music, grew infatuated with time.

EVENT HORIZON

(for Robert Pinsky, and to the memory
of Louis-Ferdinand Celine—imprisoned from
1945 to 1947, pending extradition on charges of
collaboration, in Vestre Faengsel in Copenhagen,
where a sentry did shout at him the opening line)

Hey you down there that takes it up the ass!
Ferdinand yells at me from his sentry tower
outside of it all now. Just what century

do you think you're in? *How We Became Posthuman*?
There's the Flat Stone Age, the Bone Age, the Age on its Knees,
the Age of Gunpowder—but I never mentioned

the age that sucked the universe up its tail . . .
Event Horizon! When do events stop happening?
When you've shown your waking up and your going to sleep

as well as your screwing, to everyone on your Webcam?
When the bombs no longer hurt the soldier's body,
he covers his ears with his hands, but in between

his brains have turned to jelly? Wear your wires
as if you wore your intestines on the outside,
you won't hear the train that's coming up behind you!

What's the UV forecast? What bridge collapsed, with no defect
but a hundred and forty thousand cars a day?
And don't you dare agree with me, you snotworm

who praised *soixante-huit*, then spent your whole life in school!
(And I'm him now, I'm the one below, who stumbles,
gaping through the prison chickenwire at the blue . . .)

Don't tell me they only let the ___s and the ___s
get angry in print now! I know it already! They blame
the cartoons not the rioters! not the old blind pig in the sky!

God is great! Blow up the Buddhas! Display the heads!
Blow up the Muslims too! Run your pipeline down from the Caspian!
Blood, music and lace . . . I'll show you the web of time . . . .

I don't know if your Vice President's secret phone call
meant he knew the attacks were coming, and I don't care . . .
Hide a needle in a haystack. Hide the fact

that matters among the million that might not. Shake up
the kaleidoscope all you like, it's the same shards, same dots
on your itsy-bitsy, teeny-weeny screens . . .

Oh the black weight never imagined, that sucks you under
when mind can't transmit any more . . . Yardbird, stumbling
with me in Vestre Faengsel, take your last gape at the blue

through the UV index—oh boy,
Priam, the Fates are gonna re-queer your ass!— [*Priami . . . quae fata, requiras*]
while the sentry crows! I never watched your damn screens,

Lili did, sometimes. The cheek of me, to have had That View,
the old Paris, like a fairy's wedding train,
before the bombings—the rooftops—red, black, soft gray—no
     wonder

they would have liked to push me in a wheelbarrow
over every bone-cracking cobblestone of the city
to dump me in a ditch with the other war debris,

Fartre pissing on me and screaming, "He got paid!"

BÉBERT

I walked through Hell, and didn't know it was Hell,
though I knew when an eagle was scouting the likes of me
on the banks of the Danube. My ignorance kept them sane.

When they let me loose to follow the half-witted children
through the layers of Hamburg, infolded
like plastic left on a stove, I met the man

eviscerated upright at his counter,
the hypogeum tall as a nave, the treasure-crypt
of canned goods. Many times

they gave me the meat or fish, though they ate gruel.
I learned to play dead in my sack when carried into
prisons or hospitals. At sixteen, *l'age limite*

pour un chat, I saw France again
and died. "Agile and gracious, impeccable, he still
jumped through the window that very morning . . . «

(after Frederic Vitoux, *Bébert, le chat de Louis-Ferdinand Celine*)

BAMIAN: A PHOTOGRAPH
FROM *TRICYCLE*, 2000

The boy with the beautiful face of central Asia
like an almond stood on its tip (the nose and cheek-curves
almonds within an almond) stands guarding
the almost featureless images of our larger nature,
Pheidias by way of Alexander....
Not his religion, even, but his ancestors',
and so worth respecting; worth disrespectingly, to his enemies,
because he, a Hazara, is Shiite, and they're Sunnis.
He's full-grown, and determined, but far too boyish
to be a soldier....
The semi-automatic cradled in his hands
seems hardly a weapon, capped with a pagoda-
or minaret-shaped cone.

                    Two sides of the world's vise
closing on him. Ours will be bad enough,
but for now it's benevolent, bringing medicines
and a needed witness. As for
the others...
          Genghis Khan, in his time, killed everyone
in this narrow valley. Before the end,
someone like this boy will bury the guest-books, with the names—
hippies I knew from the '60's, who smoked a bong
on the Buddha's forehead—out in a fallow field.

Hindus will spill pig's blood on the floor of a mosque in Delhi.
His tribe, returning, will bow to the empty caves.

FANTASIA ON A
MEDIEVAL LATIN POEM

Meum ist propositum
In taverna mori

Come now, don't you partly like the scene, in *Leaving Las Vegas*,
where he goes through the liquor store
and, because he'll use it to kill himself, can take one of everything:
polar vodkas, hurricane rums,
tequila of Aztec kings, slightly buttery jungle-root taste,
whiskeys of peat-fires, hickory fires, nights of wandering wind;
royal cognacs, peasant grappas,
and all the gins, snow cresting the juniper boughs . . . .

Or, as Ungaretti put it, *Ce que j'ai bu dans ma vie.*

Deus sit propitius
Huic potatori

He said it in his rooms in Leverett House—*J'ai bu de l'absinthe*—
safer, he said, than the additives in bourbon—
and liked Anne and me, because we were the only ones
to join him in a scotch at ten in the morning.
When he dozed off, Andrew Wylie, his chaperon,
motioned us all to the door.

It is my proposal
To die in a tavern

... in the moments when time has changed
to the *right* time, be it noon or midnight,
and there's no line dividing you and your life,
unless the room starts to spin ....

Top of the Sixes with Anne, the park and helicopters
below us, the city's darkening glints
like a huge globe-shaped glass she at last would share
with you .... Hangover wakings in the dark
through the years, their timeless strange warmth around your
      body ...
Wild Turkey with the Southern journalist at MacDowell,
in the little parlor, so far from home, so home,
waiting for Elaine, whom you're not sure of yet ....

Jeanne with whom the martini was reinstated,
her parents lowering the station-wagon back
on a level, almost, with the wide sun-struck bayou
(where we'd found no alligators)
for their ice-chest—chilled glasses, olives....
Two Cajuns, impassive, watched from a broken porch—

And may God be well-disposed
Unto this drinker

who fears drink, as he must, but as a god,
not "substance abuse"—
                    or, as Gary said
of Richard Hugo, "He must have seen strange things
on the way down."

NO. 1 PIAZZETTA CALAMANDREI

Lion or lamb that faced my study window—
head too effaced to tell—in the medallion
on the palazzo with the overhanging roof . . . .
Would it still ask me
the things it asked me then, across the cleft
where the sun crept down so slowly, adding only
not what have you accomplished, but have you changed?
Does being you still mean walking your own mind
as if it were a tightrope? With anger rising
against those nearest you, as if they were depriving you
of some dearest hope?
What is the thing, the flaming-up or darkening,
that brings you peace?
No answers. But why does a sudden joy
go through me, at this thinning of the veil
between me then and now?
For a moment I no longer fear the death
that waits for me,
as if it were no more than the drawing of a just sum.
Pausing, as if to enter,
my hand on the great knob of the street door . . . .

CATHEDRAL

Some days to feel like a great rock upthrusting
vertiginously hung out over miles of air,
dense with minerals, veins, all working to come forward
into the bronze explosion of the light. . . .

Others, at best, a broken-winged angel climbing
a ladder on the windy outside
of something—soul or world?—
slow, exposed rungs, imponderable rock.

LE CONVERTOIE

The name, our neighbor says, means *convergence*,
as of streams or roads—here, both. Others would have it
a contraction of *ripa moratorio*,
the cliff the convicts were thrown from to their death
when the villa was a prison.

Later, it was a school. In living memory—
the memory of those who once were taught there,
up for a Sunday stroll—
our house was where the sheep lived; where the wine-pulp
was strained through a long funnel
from what is now our kitchen to the cellar.
Later they talk—if I'm following the Italian—
about how there must always be rich and poor.

We count as the rich, though we're not the hedge-fund trader
who bought up the deconsecrated church
and put a plasma tv on the altar.

November brings hunters, with their orange vests.
They're old men, mostly, but hoard enough anger
to use passing cats for target practice,
or, when our downhill neighbor got his property
declared off limits to them, a *riserva*,
to sneak in at night and torch his cars.

Only two generations from a misery
where the only sweet was *stracchiata*
made, in the fall, from crushed grape-pulp and stale bread. . . .

But to us, the *strangers*, it's the cup of timelessness
held to our lips—
                the old people who still walk in
from the hills to the center, clutching their shopping bags,
patient as the after-echoes of a bell;
or the oak-leaves that stay red-brown instead of falling,
warming the winter woods.

OWNERSHIP

Why should I be the owner
of a stone ramp underground
with ridges hand-chiseled for the horses' hooves
back in the Middle Ages?
Or responsible as far as the small road
if stones burst from their wall in a downpour
or the wild boars get into the grapes?
Does the forest across the way eye me,
who know nothing of its depths,
with justified menace, or
a measured *let's see*, because
I have studied the painterly lines
of its trunks atilt toward each other
where the valley-sides meet at the rock?—
I whom the indecent luck
of inheritance, a lifetime's
small nudges of choice, and then
a few strokes of the pen, have made
part of the age-long
shaping of their fate—
and them, it seems, of mine.

OH THE PERSIMMONS,

not my favorite fruit,
but so triumphantly reddish,
beckoning us through the ground-mists
down to our scraggly "orchard"
to pick them
that first Christmas, when
the seller had stripped the house
even to the lighting fixtures,
so the caretaker had to give us
a few bare dangling bulbs
to see our way around by. . . .
Amidst all that, they seemed welcomers,
the first things there to tell us
we had any reason for being
there at all.

SLEEP

> Homo Fictus ... is never conceived as
> a creature a third of whose time is spent
> in the darkness.
> —E. M. Forster, *Aspects of the Novel*

Strange, how rarely it's a topic. Yet how we cherish that dark,
soothing lake water beneath our chattery
reflexive surfaces.
         "Already," a story has it,
"she seemed to be fishing in her night's sleep."
And doesn't that get it perfectly?—the heaviness
that pulls luxuriously slowly from the forehead
into the eyes the sign that somewhere
a dream has struck the line ....

         Happy too, perhaps,
because in that moment we could be anywhere
we've been in that moment.
         The IC train
every twenty minutes. If I'm still awake after ten
my mother's bathwater running in the tap
across the wall from my ear.
         Utterly
safe, because utterly undefended.

◆

When Gilgamesh sails beyond the world's end to Utnapishtim,
the one immortal man, Noah of the Babylonian Flood,

to ask how he himself could live forever,
the test Utnapishtim sets him

is to stay awake six days and nights on end.
Of course he fails, and tries to lie about it,

sleep coming over him as irresistibly
as ocean mist comes over the shore from the waters.

Then Utnapishtim spoke to his wife and said:
"See how this hero sleeps who asks for life."

◆

I'll never make anything so intricate
in thought or poetry, as the things I make
in sleep—
           driving through mountains
I've never seen, in Montana, to an exact
small town; the rearrangements of Berkeley,
adding new freeways and goatpaths, the wide prow
of steps on the bank/courthouse that now divides
the top of University. . . .
                  Plato or Olivier
Messiaen might have found in this an argument
for the literalness of heaven, arising
out of the final sleep
like a city rising from water, built by music . . . .

Though one could put the question another way: just what
is missing in us, that needs so many worlds?

◆

And how we're scared when sleep doesn't come—Plath's simile
of the nights snapping out of sight like a lizard's eyelid;

or how, as a child, I said *Let's explore the night*
to cheer myself, but felt that eerie ringing

like a tin fork struck repeatedly on a tin pan,
the atmosphere of some strange planet where I was exiled,

the ship that marooned me receding but not vanishing . . . .
And of course we try: breathe slowly long enough,

you can almost stop thought—let an image come instead . . . .
Maybe it works; or hours pass, and we know

you can clear away anything but a transparency.

◆

The Medici tombs. Dusk's penis, an embodiment
of gravity, flat on the inner thigh.
His face's stone left vague, as if to tell us
he no longer cares if what he has done in the world
is good or bad, distinguished or worthless.
                                        Opposite him
Dawn in pain, her eyelids closed but tensed, her neck
torqued sideways and up, in the great struggle between
the call of morning and the wish for sleep . . . .

Seduction of Night, her Eve-like triangular head, her owl
and tragic mask with teeth . . . .

(Day and Night for the man of action, Dawn and Dusk
for the man of thought . . . .)

Standing before them, my face would show the same
tense transparency, almost an old man,
as when I came there at twenty—round eye
almost equaling the round chamber . . . .
                                        This is what
exalts and terrifies.
                        When I have come there
for the last time, will there be a sum
of all the viewings, an understanding on the edge
waving farewell?—or just blurred

collapse, Dusk's penis, an embodiment . . . .

                        ◆

Sleep that knits up . . . .

                        Theo Carlton my cat
has a different relation; he's in and out of it
the whole sunstruck day, both in and out of our company,
of the dazzling world's.
                                He registers, here, his gratitude
for my bad sinuses, overdrinking, or whatever
can make me, too, tired of being awake by noon—

though with no illusion that such down-payments to uncon-
        sciousness
will postpone the due-date of Utnapishtim's judgment:

See how this hero sleeps who asks for life.

MESSENGERS FROM THE PAST

Overplaying like competing radio stations,
static of shame and loss and self-revulsion
making the present moment
briefly unlivable—
these outsize simultaneities of the past . . . .

Or, more august but hardly more bearable, they rush toward us
with the knowledge of repetition
becoming Fate, like the four naked horsemen
converging toward the painted
door of the death-realm in the tombs at Tarquinia.

Door into depthless stone. And still, there are times
when simultaneity seems completeness: my friend's head,
young at being old
after his winter reading in Chicago,
held all the moments I'd known him, the gray

only molding, clarifying
the intention of his youthful gaze: like the egg
the Etruscan holds up joyfully—
not "resurrection" perhaps, but surely "the germ" of everything—
between thumb and forefinger at his own funeral banquet.

THE OLD MAN BY THE ROADSIDE

—no, crossing the road slowly, ignoring the cars,
with an implement in his hand—a motorized
lawn-edge trimmer, perhaps, on a long pole—
something that probably hadn't existed when he was a boy
and seemed too big for him now, requiring balance....
His gauntness stood out so, in that moment,
in the very late afternoon sun—as if, I thought,
the wrinkling of the neck-skin, drawing in on
the tendons tightening and standing out,
were the visible sign of existence withdrawing
a portion of its knowledge—knowledge, perhaps, of the year
when the boars were all eaten and the vipers thrived,
when German tanks rolled down the dirt roads, and Partisans
were shot at places that would be marked with crosses
you came on in the deep woods, in the future years....
Would he have been a participant, or just a witness
as a frightened child? Whichever, when he goes,
when all his kind are gone, when the shrinking
will have reached the bones and eventually the heart,
all that will no longer be life but hearsay.
Fictive almost, to the ones I'm old enough to think
cut off from the real, behind their screens
of diffracting marvels... But their knowledge
will be life, too; will change with age; and will be gone.

LEOPARDI: CHORUS OF THE DEAD

The one eternal thing
in this world, to which
every created being
must return—in you,
Death, our naked nature
finds repose,
not happy, but secure
from ancient torment. Night,
profoundest night, obscures
our minds; we have no thought
of our predicament.
As for desire and hope,
the arid spirit lacks breath.
Without anguish and fear,
without tedium, the empty
slow centuries pass. We lived.
And as a nursing child
confusedly remembers
some fear in the night—a spectre,
or a dream he woke from, sweating—
that's how our time alive
presents itself. But why
we were afraid escapes
us. What were we?
What was that bitter apex
called life? Arcane
and overpowering
it seems to us, as death,
the Unknown, in the thoughts

of the living. And as in life
it fled from death, just so
in death our naked nature
dreads the living flame—
not happy, but secure,
since fate
denies beatitude
alike to the living and to the dead.

THE BHARHUT GATE

"If you cannot endure this moment, what can you endure?"   (Kyoto)
it asks, in English as well as Japanese,
just as you enter the courtyard of raked sand
with two perfect cones at the center—
Daitoku–ji's bristling, blackish Northern wood
dragon-curved, fish-scaled: the haunted spirit's
battle-castles....

        But later on the day
will blossom out, like a perfect day from childhood,
white plum and old boats sinking
into amber lagoons.

        There is
a continuity-line, as the guide would say, days later
before the Bharhut Gate, in the Museum,   (Calcutta)
showing how the stories connect, a grapevine ending
somewhere in an elephant's mouth, or a man's navel. . . .

When the secret agent in the movie finger-tests
the layer of dust on her new desk, that's my
first touch of Calcutta—not the broken sidewalks,
the broken beggars reclined on their blankets astride them,
the thick red curtains that pass for luxury, full of dust. . . .

But the Bharhut Gate is shining: the red-bronze sandstone
so polished I took it for a replica
the first time round. The grapevine-umbilicus
joins everything. Onlookers crowd

carved windows. Fish turn into elephants
above the waist. (The lower life
turning into the higher?) There's an equally
mercurial emphasis on *jataka*, reincarnations....

Oh cavort through your other lives, in their leafiness,
be a monkey amid the green, and make your body
a bridge between two trees, the other monkeys
can cross and escape the hunters...
                                But the Buddha as himself
is empty, represented only by his footprints
in these early sculptures. Time being presented
side-by-side here, he mounts into it, leaving
his household; we see first an empty chariot,
then a riderless horse, finally just
the footprints.

        So, perhaps, my daughter and I,
triumphantly scared, as the train carried us
past laborers bathing in the ponds at twilight
into a total dark like the Middle Ages....

Someone met us, with our names on a placard, at the station;   (GAYA)
we survived. But as the central stupa
the gate surrounded must be imagined, now,
the pilgrimage blurs. A dog sniffed my hand,
a monk took my picture, and I didn't know it,
as I meditated, not, I thought, that profoundly,
under the railing at Bodh Gaya.

               I too took pictures.
When the goats broke so perfectly across
the rectilinear ruins, I asked our guide
if he thought the goatherd would mind being photographed.

"It's the only way he'll ever get to America!"
the guide laughed. And here he is, on my wall,
in his blue-green plastic sunhat....

And the Buddha becomes human, if androgynous,   (VARANASI)
from Sarnath on. It's as if such a symmetry fell
on closed eyes and cheekbones, the mouth could not help turning
up in a faint smile, despite all that ends
in smoke, at the burning ghats.
  Oh rake the dust
and make a perfect cone! The way the Taj   (AGRA)
seen from behind the crowds pressing darkly
toward the dark entrance-archway floated, free
of gravity almost, in a luminousness,
a white nimbus, that would not return
when I stood numbering the intricate
bits of *pietra dura*—countless as sand, or dust...

"If you cannot endure this moment, what can you endure?"

MONTALE AT MONTEROSSO

You came to a place
where, like the agave stretching from the cliff-face,
you saw your own small heart
mirrored in a vaster one;
where every doubt that frightened you
could be led along
like a friendly child by the hand.
You were so near the origins
you had taken off your face.
You saw some sea-bird
fly on, under the fixed blue,
without pausing, because on every image is written
"deeper in."

(derived from the poems "L'Agave sullo scoglio" and "Portovenere")

II.

FRANCISCAN NOTES

Man can embody truth, but he cannot know it.
—W. B. YEATS

[Much of the structure of this sequence derives
from Olivier Messiaen's opera *St. Francois d'Assise,*
hence the references to the *ondes martenot,* an
early type of electronic instrument, and other
peculiarities of Messiaen's music. But all the
stories Messiaen tells can also be found in the
Little Flowers of Saint Francis.]

1. UPPER CHURCH

Let the notes begin, and the blue:
xylophone, glockenspiel, celeste
one lonely violin
and the spook-house whoosh of the *ondes martenot*. . . .

And the starry blue, that protects
not only Mary
sidesaddle on her donkey into Egypt,
but this man, cauterized by Brother Fire,

who says—the music driving
like hard rain—that if, unrecognized,
soaked with mud, tormented by hunger,
he was beaten and driven away
from his own cloister, into the roaring night,

and he accepted it,
that would be perfect joy;
and who becomes (in spite
or because of this?)

our model of transparence toward all that is.

2. LOWER CHURCH

Dread advances. Wedded to stone.
Cringing against the pedestals soaring.

How can they be so tall then, and the vault
so very, very low?

Once I walked into daylight, but the stones called to me,
only we will rock you lovingly, after you're dead.

If their converging weight could press the juice
out of me, to express

the bottom of things. . . . But I can only expel it
by gestures, cries, or spasms. I impel it.

If there were a crack in the stones, it would only let
what's left of me seep out, or a greater nothingness enter.

Be very still then. Stiller
than an egg. Brother Leo

is still nearby, not buried alive; and somewhere
a ghostly flight of snowy plovers skims the sand.

Twice, conquering, I've crossed over.

3. BLACK CRUCIFIXION

Not earthquake but oxidation has exploded
these figures
to a negative of themselves, black at the center,
ghostly gold trace at the rims—
such as the end will make of all of us.

But also the beginning. Working by smoky flax—
the cavern's roof a grave's
six inches above him—someone, lying there,
found it held latent in its nubs and ridging
the flair of his kingly companions, cave-bear, ibex—

4. BLESSING OF THE ANIMALS

Oh you who preached to the double orchestra
half-hidden in the round tree,

consider, if you will, a little namesake,
Leo, who found the *querencia* of his dying
in the violently tall white stand of summer grass
at the back of the neighbors' yard.
He lay there all day, waiting.
What were his thoughts? Was it for himself
or for us, he came back, when we called at twilight,
his poor cancerous paw swollen to double size?

(Then flew away, into the four directions,
making the sign of the Cross.)

5. THE PLUNGE

Of the weeks after my mother's death
I remember fragments. Landing in Italy.
Huddling in the inmost corner
of a stone bench inside our fireplace,
as if its embers
held the only, tiny warmth left in the world. . . .

La Verna. Francis's cave.
Slants of green light down
through the rocks. The bed
of stone where the saint had slept,
an iron grille across it, to prevent the pious
from lying down there.

I fell. I stood there, but I fell
an age, a moment's blackness,
onto the knobby stone.
When I came to myself, there was joy.

I could walk out into daylight.

Afterwards, inside the monastic corridors,
I sat down somewhere. The late afternoon sun
gathered, through a narrow window, on my head.
Later I learned
it was the same place Bonaventure sat
when he was given *The Mind's Road to God*.

6. THE MIND'S ROAD TO GOD

Do I believe the seraph with six wings
that gave Francis the wounds
gave Bonaventure his system?

(Do I believe Francis's flesh
took on the shape
not only of the wound, but of the nail?)

The mind's road a fantastic
series of receding mirrors....

Meditating in that corner,
he delighted in the things of this world
but found he saw them from a greater distance,

tracing the source of their beauty
to number and proportion,
so leaving the realm of place, time, and motion
for what is unchangeable, illimitable, without end.

But it was by retreating into itself
the mind looked upon God in the brightness of the saints,
discerning that its own three faculties,
memory, intelligence, and love,
mirrored the Trinity....

Meditating in that corner,
he finds his mind is lost at last, adoring
the contradictions of the three-in-one,
a God of "the greatest mutual intimacy"
who is also God on a "mission. . . ."

—Ineffable, or scholastic logic-chopping?

But this: *"So great*
is the force of the highest good
that nothing can be loved
except through desire for it."

7. COUNTERTHEME

> Except to express a terrible feeling of fear or anxiety,
> I see no emotion in this music
> > —*Olivier Messiaen, on why he used the*
> > *twelve-tone scale only in the scene of the*
> > *Stigmata*

Paralyzed by the snake's eye of approaching age
I lived inertly.

All the notes the same, whatever their order.

The first nail was the sun, locking me
in a world of things that die.

The second nail was dust,
rising from all of those things.

The last nails were having to be
in only one place at one time.

This morning square, famous for its beauty.

◆

But when you are lifted up on the wood
(one painter saw)

angles and lucid polygons unfold
unknown dimensions.

I know their lesson: if you can consent
to a moment, unknowingly,

the worlds move forward with you....
I *know*: all that for now

seems words, seems out of reach.

8. KNOCK AT THE DOOR

The knock is always
amplified.
That's how you know it's the angel,
even if it's only Jeanne
finding too many problems with the house
our first morning in Italy.
You can respond with anger
like Brother Elias,
or be glad to be summoned back
to ponder your own and others'
freedom or predestination.

9. A BLESSING OF PLANTS

Spring returns. You can put sorrel and lovage in salads.
Even an old man might be happy to be alive,

and wonder what the textures, close up
under his paring-knife,
carrot, fine-grained as wood,
but a grain of water-beads,
potatoes and turnips a pearl's smoothness and glow
with an un-pearl-like softness,

had to do with that theory
that the universe
is all the frequencies of a single string.

10. ON A BEACH IN WESTERN AUSTRALIA

Bacterial mud-towers, first life-forms.
They released oxygen. All the oceans rusted.

Where wast thou when I laid the foundations of the earth?

11. JOY, FALL

Joy fall to thee, father Francis,
Drawn to the Life that died

not once and historically, as you believed,
but omnipresent:

cold damp to the core of all bones
in the Umbrian winter;
one wolf frightening a whole city;
surgery by white-hot iron,
lepers public entertainment
for those at the peepholes into the sanitorium—

and half of Europe killed off
a bare century later—

and you not repelled but
drawn to it,
          skull
and beatific face.

12. TRANSPARENCE

Something strange happened in me once.
An axis in my mind shifted
as I'm told certain electrons do, under strain,
from up versus down to back versus front.
Behind in the cavern were those dragons
who do not permit
anything that contradicts them to be believed.
Ahead, the day open, like my daughter's face.

Is this his transparence,
when the angel sings from beyond the window,
and pain and shame, even of being a leper,
can be understood as
Your heart condemns you,
and answered, *God is bigger than your heart?*

But so hard to stay turned outward,
especially on the edge of being exceedingly happy,
that being beaten and driven away
from the monastery into the roaring night
might just be a metaphor. . . .

I think what I say is true
because in telling of it I feel
my joy expand . . .

        O plunge
and uprush on the xylophone and strings!

13. THE GUIDE

Someone said: no one has proved that consciousness
and the brain are identical.

A doctor lay in a coma. No signals from the neocortex,
the place where our humanity,

language, thought, emotion, all reside.
But somewhere, he was led

through a cave realm, where roots a little
like blood vessels, glowing a dirty red,

reached far above and below,
and shapes jostled him, turning to half-human faces;

led, then, through regions of increasing light,
flocks of cloud-like transparent orbs,

by a companion, a young woman
who spoke to him in an accent combining

and transcending every form of love—
romantic, friendly, maternal—

to a place where his questions were answered
almost before he had posed them.

The parallel too obvious to be stated.

My own hope has not been to live again
but to experience some resolution, or clarification,

of our long struggle with ourselves and fate,
not the good and the bad cut off with the same blunt stroke.

I can't persuade anyone it will happen,
any more than the doctor, or Dante, could.

But the guide—you know who you are—

14. AFTERWORD

At my memorial service, please play Francis's
Farewell to the Earth,
not because
I am in the least like Francis,
but because it is
farewell to the earth.

ACKNOWLEDGMENTS

Poems from this collection appeared in the following periodicals, and are reprinted with gratitude:

Agni: "Event Horizon," "Bebert," "Poems of Summer"

The American Scholar: "A Sick Child," "After Oral Surgery," "Summer Afternoon in the South," "The Bharhut Gate"

Arts & Letters: "The Psychopomps"

Christianity and Literature: "Franciscan Notes" 1, 2, and 4

Literary Imagination: "Jojo Listens to Gotterdammerung," "New Orleans Poem"

Northwest Review: "The Death of Picasso," "Fantasia on a Medieval Latin Poem"

Ploughshares: "For My Mother," "Sleep"

Seizure State: "After Caravaggio," "Cathedral"

Slate: "No. 1 Piazzetta Calamandrei"

Tikkun: "Bamian: A Photograph from TriCycle"

The Yale Review: "San Francisco Grand Ball, Airport Marriott," "The Ring," "The Old Man by the Roadside"

"Franciscan Notes," sections 1-8, also appeared in an Italian translation by Bianca Tarozzi, in *Smerilliana*.

ABOUT THE AUTHOR

ALAN WILLIAMSON was born in Chicago in 1944, and educated at Haverford and Harvard. He has taught at the University of Virginia, Harvard, Brandeis, and the University of California, Davis, where he retired as Distinguished Professor in 2013. He is an ongoing faculty member in the Warren Wilson MFA Program for Writers. He has won fellowships from the National Endowment for the Arts and the Guggenheim Foundation; and has been a poetry panelist for the NEA and for the Pulitzer Prize.

Williamson's five books of literary criticism cover topics as wide-ranging as the political vision of Robert Lowell; male writers and female identification; and literature and painting in the American West. His volumes of poetry are *Presence* (Knopf, 1983), *The Muse of Distance* (Knopf, 1988), *Love and the Soul* (University of Chicago Press, 1995), *Res Publica* (Chicago, 1998), and *The Pattern More Complicated: New and Selected Poems* (Chicago, 2004). His long-standing interest in Italy and Italian literature led to a complete translation of Cesare Pavese's last volume, *Death Will Come and Look at Me with Your Eyes*, published in *The American Poetry Review*, and later to *The Living Theatre: Selected Poems of Bianca Tarozzi*, co-translated with Jeanne Foster (BOA, 2017). *The Living Theatre* won the Bay Area Book Reviewers Award for poetry in translation in 2018.

CPSIA information can be obtained
at www.ICGtesting.com
Printed in the USA
FSHW011812280919

9 781946 482259